A special dedication to my father, Antonio
Baldonado, who died last year.

mentoring

v. imp to guide
& support through
their career.

25 Ways
To Motivate Generation Y:

A Pocketbook Guide

personal life v important

- address approach to
  delegation, task allocation
  & time mgt

- need responsibility &
  growth (inc skill & knowled[ge]

- work condition v. important

- employers approach to
  mge & policies etc.
      - flexibility

- WLB - flexible working
      - benefits pkg - gyms
                        etc

Backspace set up is very in line with motivating Gen Y.

— become to expect it !

— should still be personal & not sheep dipped

25 Ways
To Motivate Generation Y:

A Pocketbook Guide

Arthur M. Baldonado, Ph.D.

iUniverse, Inc.
New York   Bloomington

25 Ways to Motivate Generation Y: A Pocketbook Guide

iUniverse books may be ordered through booksellers or by contacting:

iUniverse
1663 Liberty Drive
Bloomington, IN 47403
www.iuniverse.com
1-800-Authors (1-800-288-4677)

ISBN: 978-1-4401-0544-9 (pbk)
ISBN: 978-1-4401-0545-6 (ebk)

Printed in the United States of America

iUniverse rev. date: 10/22/08

Acknowledgement

This book would not have been possible without the help and guidance of the following individuals:

I would like to express my deepest gratitude to my alma mater, Northcentral University, and my dissertation committee for their guidance and support: Dr. Janice M. Spangenburg (chair), Dr. Rocky J. Dwyer, Dr. Marie Gould, and Dr. William Welsh III.

To my editors, Shawn Stewart, Tina Pedersen and Sandra Dawson for their tireless efforts in reviewing my work.

To the seminal/inspirational work of the following researchers/authors: Dr. Carolyn A. Martin, Mr. Bruce Tulgan, Ms. Lynne C. Lancaster, and Mr. David Stillman. Their work on Gen Y truly inspired me to pursue my doctoral studies on Gen Y cohort.

I would also like to thank all the students and faculty members at the University of Hawaii campus, and Dr. Jaysun Chun, who participated/supported me in my dissertation/survey.

To the staff of IUniverse—thanks for making this book and my dream come true.

Finally, a special thanks to my family who provided their love and support during this incredible endeavor/journey—my wife Emily and son Zachary Baldonado. To my mother, Aurora Baldonado; parent-in-law Lisa and Gerry Garcenila; sisters Aura Hampton and Aileen Morado—thanks for all your love & support. Without each one of you, I could not have achieved all my dreams.

Preface

This book is based on my dissertation study and research of Gen Y at Northcentral University entitled "Exploring the Workplace Motivational and Managerial Factors Associated with Gen Y." My dissertation was a qualitative, descriptive research study designed to explore the motivational needs of Gen Y and their impact in the workplace based on Herzberg's two-factor theory of motivation. With the support and authorization of the University of Hawaii system, a researcher-designed, written questionnaire was administered to students in a business class at the University of Hawaii campus. The findings of the study revealed that Gen Y cohort placed great importance to both hygiene and motivator factors in their motivational needs. Growth and personal life were both important to Gen Y students.

Although this book is about motivating Gen Y in the workplace, the content is applicable to all ages in the workforce. It is geared for managers and supervisors of all younger workers. I hope this book will assist readers in understanding the basic motivational needs of Gen Y workers. The author listed 25 ways to motivate Gen Y workers. The list is not all inclusive. There are more unique ways to motivate younger workers, and this list is a good starting point.

Part I defined Gen Y in the workplace. Gen Ys are individuals born after 1980. Part II provided four motivational theories pertinent to motivating younger workers. Part III described the author's dissertation study. Part IV provided 25 ways to motivate Gen Y workers. Finally, Part V provided closing remarks on motivating Gen Y members in the workplace.

Contents

- Involvement in decisions-
- family discussions
- thrive on flexibility

PART I:
GEN Y DEFINED

Known as "Nexters" (Schlichtemeier-Nutzman, 2002, p. 35) because they are the next wave of employees and "Echo Boomers" (p. 36) because they are similar to their Baby Boomer predecessor's in size, Gen Y, individuals born after 1980, began entering the workplace during the summer of 2000. Gen Y is 81 million strong, comprising 30% of the current United States population (Dulin, 2005). With very focused and involved Boomer parents, Gen Y grew up with busy schedules—sports, music lessons, and scheduled play-dates occupying much of their time. Gen Y always had input in family decisions because their parents constantly communicated with them (Lancaster & Stillman, 2002). Despite some variations in the way researchers and experts name and classify start and end dates (i.e., Gen Y end dates of 1977), there is a general descriptive consensus among academics and practitioners regarding Gen Y (Eisner, 2005).

Gen Yers are independent, techno-savvy, and entrepre-neurial employees who thrive on flexibility (Martin, & Tulgan, 2001). In their book entitled Managing Generation Y: Global Citizens Born in the Late Seventies and Early Eighties, Martin and Tulgan listed the following as the truths about Gen Y:

1. A generation of new confidence, upbeat and full of self-esteem — *motivation*
2. The most education minded generation in history — *learning*
3. A generation paving the way to a more open, tolerant society
4. A generation leading a new wave of volunteerism

In the workplace, Gen Y appears to be more idealistic than Generation X, but a little bit more realistic than Baby Boomers. Researchers describe Gen Y as "considerably more optimistic and more interested in volunteerism than Generation X" (Schlichtemeier-Nutzman, 2002, p. 49). Global communication and access to instant information via the World Wide Web have influenced the beliefs and expectations of Gen Y and has directly transform Gen Y's attitudes toward work, work ethics, values, job expectations, and overall job satisfaction (Martin & Tulgan, 2001). Schlichtemeier-Nutzman (2002) noted that the scope of Gen Y's potential impact is still being studied as they have begun entering the workforce.

World events shaping Gen Y worldview include the Columbine school shootings, President Clinton and Monica Lewinsky, and the terrorist attacks on September 11, 2001 (Meredith et al., 2002; Zemke et al., 2000). However, perhaps what best defines Gen Y at this stage in their lives is their comfort and familiarity with technology— the Internet (Meredith et al., 2002; Martin & Tulgan, 2001; Zemke et al., 2000). Born into a wired world, Gen Y is able to adapt effortlessly to advancements and have always known the Internet, computers, cell phones, VCRs, laser surgery, and genetic engineering (Smola & Sutton, 2002; Zemke et al., 2000; Strauss & Howe, 1991). Some of the well-known Gen Yers include Britney Spears, Chelsea Clinton, and Miley Cyrus (Biography.com, 2007).

GEN Y AT A GLANCE

Age	<ul><li>Gen Y includes individuals born after 1980 to 2000</li><li>Approximately 81 million people belong to this cohort</li><li>Gen Y is more than three times the size of Gen X</li></ul>
Ethnicity	<ul><li>Gen Y is the most ethnically diverse generation to date</li><li>One out of every three Gen Y members is not Caucasian</li><li>Nine out of ten children under 12 have friends outside their own ethnicity</li></ul>
Home	<ul><li>One out of four lives in a single parent household</li><li>Three out of four have working mothers</li><li>The child is the center of the household</li></ul>
Money	<ul><li>One out of nine high schoolers have credit cards co-signed by a parent</li><li>Teens have an average of $100/week disposable income</li><li>40% of teens have a part-time job</li></ul>
Connectivity	<ul><li>Gen Y seems to be less cynical and more concerned w/ social issues than Gen X, although whether to act on those feelings is always a question</li><li>75%-90% have a computer at home</li><li>50% have Internet access at home</li></ul>
Interaction	<ul><li>Gen Y prefer directness over subtlety, action over observation and coolness over all else</li><li>They are heavily influenced by their peers and the media</li><li>Although technically advanced and saturated, they would prefer personal contact</li></ul>
Status	<ul><li>Gen Y feel crunched for time, always in a hurry</li><li>Gen Y have direction and know what they want</li></ul>

Weakness	▪ Some Yers lack direction/focus/ confidence as well as interpersonal/ soft skills
Assets	▪ Educated/experienced/sociable/ technical/perform/work ethic/ multitask
Style	▪ Get done/fast-paced/open and civic-minded/blend work and play
Qualities	▪ Large size/diverse/skilled/energetic/ socially conscious/demanding
Value	▪ Heroism/virtue/duty/family/service/ work to live norm
Formative Events	▪ Prosperity/uncertainty/violence/ terrorism/outsourcing

Source: NAS Insights (2006). Generation Y: The millennials, ready or not, here they come

PART II:
WORK MOTIVATION
THEORIES

Four motivation theories were discussed in the study: Maslow's Hierarchy of Needs, Herzberg's Motivator-Hygiene theory, Vroom's Expectancy theory, and Hackman-Oldham Model.

Maslow's Hierarchy of Needs. For half a century, Maslow's classic theory has fueled research on motivation and has been a cornerstone of many motivational studies (Janiszewski, 2004). Maslow (1968) posits that when a lower need is fulfilled, it is no longer motivational and a higher need takes its place. In brief, Maslow proposed five distinct types of needs that motivate human behavior: physiological, safety, love, esteem, and self-actualization. Physiological needs are the hierarchy's lower needs such as hunger and thirst while safety needs are second-level which relate to the acquisition of objects/relationships that protect their possessor from future threats. In addition, love needs are third-level which include the need for family and friendships while esteem needs are fourth-level which include respect, feeling of appreciation, and self-esteem. Finally, self-actualization is the top-level and is defined as the person's desire to realize his or her full potential (Wagner & Hollenbeck, 2001).

Wagner and Hollenbeck (2001) summed the importance and criticism of Maslow's Hierarchy of Needs:

Perhaps owing to its simplicity, Maslow's need theory has gained wide acceptance among managers and management educators. Maslow failed to provide researchers with clear-cut measures of his concepts, however, and his theory has not received much empirical support. It holds interest for us primarily because of its place in history as one of the earliest motivation models and as a precursor to more modern theories of motivation. (p. 105)

Herzberg's Motivator-Hygiene Theory. Herzberg (1968) developed the motivator/hygiene theory or two-factor theory. Herzberg began his research in the mid-1950s by surveying 200 engineers and accountants for framework around their motivators (Wagner & Hollenbeck, 2001). By combining his findings with other researchers using different frameworks, Herzberg developed a model of motivation on the assumption that factors eliciting job satisfaction and motivation are independent from those producing job dissatisfaction.

The two-factor theory assumes that factors producing job satisfaction (motivators, or intrinsic rewards) differ from those producing job dissatisfaction (hygiene factors, or extrinsic rewards). The motivators are "achievement, recognition for achievement, the work itself, responsibility, and growth or advancement" (Herzberg, 1968, p. 91-92). The hygiene or dissatisfaction-avoidance factors, which are extrinsic to the job, include "company policy and administration, supervision, interpersonal relationships, working conditions, salary, status, and security" (Herzberg, p. 92).

Herzberg (1968) concluded that removing hygiene factors did not guarantee employee satisfaction, but simply brought peace within an organization and does not motivate employees.

Satisfaction is only increased with motivators, suggesting job roles should be redefined to increase recognition, responsibility, achievement, and advancement.

Vroom's Expectancy Theory. Vroom (1964) examined motivation in the perspective of why individuals choose to follow a particular course of action. Vroom's expectancy theory, or VIE theory include three major components: Valence—the amount of satisfaction that an individual achieves, receiving from a particular outcome; Instrumentality—a person's subjective belief about the relationship between performing a behavior and receiving an outcome; Expectancy—a person's belief regarding the link between one's efforts and his or her performance (Wagner & Hollenbeck, 2001).

Vroom (1964) suggested that a worker's beliefs about VIE interact psychologically to create a motivation force resulting in the following formula: [Motivation = Valence x Expectancy (Instrumentality)]. In addition, Vroom noted that motivation is based on unique individual factors such as personality, skills, knowledge, experience, and abilities (Wagner & Hollenbeck, 2001). Wagner and Hollenbeck summed up the importance of valence theory.

> Thus expectancy theory defines motivation in terms of desire and effort, whereby the achievement of desired outcomes results from the interaction of valences, instrumentalities, and expectancies. Desire arises only when both valence and instrumentality are high, and effort comes about when all three aspects are high. (p. 102)

Hackman-Oldham Model. Hackman and Oldham (1980) examined worker's motivation and found that work is experienced as more meaningful when employees are capable of accomplishing their jobs (Burnes, 2006). According to the Hackman-Oldham model, jobs are likely to motivate performance and contribute to employee satisfaction, and jobs must exhibit the following five core job characteristics:

skill variety, task identity, task significance, autonomy, and feedback (Wagner & Hollenbeck, 2001). Wagner and Hollenbeck provided the following definitions for the five core job characteristics:

1) Skill variety: The degree to which a jobholder must carry out a variety of activities and use a number of different personal skills in performing the job.
2) Task identity: The degree to which performing a job results in the completion of a whole and identifiable piece of work and a visible outcome that can be recognized as the result of personal performance.
3) Task significance: The degree to which a job has a significant effect on the lives of other people, whether those people are coworkers in the same firm or other individuals in the surrounding environment.
4) Autonomy: The degree to which the jobholder has the freedom, independence, and discretion necessary to schedule work and to decide which procedures to use in carrying out that work.
5) Feedback: The degree to which performing the activities required by the job provides the worker with the direct and clear information about the effectiveness of his or her performance. (p. 179)

Subsequently, the five-core job characteristic influences the extent to which workers experience three critical psychological states or personal, internal reactions to their jobs: experienced meaningfulness of work, experienced responsibility for outcomes of work, and knowledge of the actual results of work activities. If employees experienced all these states simultaneously, four kinds of work and personal outcomes are likely to result: high internal work motivation, high-quality work performance, high satisfaction with work, and low absenteeism and turnover. Finally, the following moderators or individual difference determines whether the Hackman-Oldham motivation model will lead to the preferred outcomes as indicated previously: knowledge and skill, growth-need strength, and context satisfactions (Wagner & Hollenbeck, 2001).

All four motivation theories discussed are effective in explaining workers' motivational needs. There are a myriad of motivational theories in the literature. The abovementioned motivational theories are a good starting point in understanding the basic needs of workers.

PART III:
THE STUDY

This author seeks to explore the workplace motivational factors and provide winning strategies in strengthening job satisfaction of Gen Y. The research is based on the author's dissertation study on exploring the workplace motivation factors associated with Gen Y. In reviewing the existing literature, some 150 articles were located on-line through academic databases including ProQuest and FirstSearch using "Gen Y," "Workplace," and "Motivation" as search terms locators.

The following research questions were used to guide the qualitative descriptive study of Generation Y workplace motivational factors based on Herzberg's two-factor theory model with students at the University of Hawaii:

1. What motivator factors help motivate Gen Y employees in the workplace?
2. What hygiene factors help motivate Gen Y employees in the workplace?
3. What strategies can managers provide to strengthen job satisfaction of Gen Y employees?

This qualitative, descriptive research study was designed to explore the motivational needs of Gen Y and their impact in the workplace. With the support and authorization of the

University of Hawaii system, a researcher-designed, written questionnaire was administered to students in a business class at the University of Hawaii campus. The first part of the questionnaire contained demographic information to discriminate for students who are born after 1980. The second section of the questionnaire contained opinion-based questions on the motivational factors affecting Generation Y, using Hertzberg two-factor theory. Using summary statistics, the responses to a Likert-type scale were analyzed. The results of the study are intended to provide a body of knowledge relating to the motivational and management needs of Gen Y. The need for this study is significant and useful for management in helping analyze the motivational and management needs of Gen Y (Dulin, 2005; Smola & Sutton, 2002).

Survey Result

The researcher sought to determine the importance of the 16-hygiene/motivator factors of Herzberg's two-factor theory of motivation (1968) and asked participants to rate each factor. The following five-point Likert scale were offered to survey respondents: very important, important, moderately important, little importance, and not important. Nineteen students participated in the survey, and all were members of Gen Y. Table 1 depicts the results of the survey based on median, mode, and mean.

Table 1. Mean, Median, & Mode of the Survey
16-Hygiene/Motivator Factors – Mean, Median, & Mode

Achievement	Mean=1.89	Mode=1	Median=2
Security	Mean=2.15	Mode=2	Median=2
Recognition	Mean=2.1	Mode=2	Median=2
Status	Mean=2.42	Mode=3	Median=2
Work itself	Mean=2	Mode=2	Median=2
Relationship with subordinates	Mean=1.84	Mode=2	Median=2
Responsibility	Mean=1.9	Mode=2	Median=3
Personal life	Mean=1.36	Mode=1	Median=2
Advancement	Mean=2	Mode=2	Median=2
Relationship with peers	Mean=1.8	Mode=2	Median=2
Growth	Mean=1.73	Mode=2	Median=2
Salary	Mean=1.68	Mode=1	Median=2
Work conditions	Mean=1.42	Mode=1	Median=2
Relationship with supervisor	Mean=1.73	Mode=2	Median=2
Supervision	Mean=32	Mode=3	Median=2
Company policy and admin	Mean=2.26	Mode=2	Median=2
Other	n/a		

Discussion

Upon analyzing Gen Y responses to the survey, it was clear that this cohort had distinct motivation/hygiene needs. Responses to the survey indicated Gen Y placed great importance to both hygiene and motivator factors. However, a few factors stood out among the others. The 16 hygiene/

motivator factors received an average mean of 1.92. Table 2 shows the perceived overall ranking of Herzberg's two-factor theory of motivation based on mean value.

Table 2. Gen Y Perceived Overall Ranking (Two-Factor Theory)

1) Personal life (M=1.36)
2) Working conditions (M=1.42)
3) Salary (M=1.68)
4) Relationship w/ supervisor (M=1.73)
Tied at 4) Growth (M=1.73)
5) Relationship w/ peers (M=1.8)
6) Relationship w/ subordinates (M=1.84)
7) Achievement (M=1.89)
8) Responsibility (M=1.9)
9) Advancement (M=2)
Tied at 9) Work itself (M=2)
10) Recognition (M=2.1)
11) Security (M=2.15)
12) Company policy/admin (M=2.26)
13 Status (M=2.42)
14) Supervision (M=2.52)

The first research question addressed by the researcher in this investigation was *What motivator factors help motivate Gen Y employees in the workplace?* Herzberg (1968) identified the following as motivator factors: growth, achievement, responsibility, achievement, advancement, work itself, and recognition. The response to the survey indicated Gen Y members rated growth, achievement, and responsibility as important motivator factors to their motivational needs.

GROWTH + achievement *(handwritten)*

Among the motivator factors, Gen Y survey participants placed the highest importance on growth needs. A high percentage of students (63%) indicated growth in one's career as important. No students believed growth as having little or no importance. Similarly, students indicated achievement and responsibility as important motivator factors. When asked to rate the statement, "Having achieved something at work motivates me," a vast majority of respondents (42%) indicated achievement at work as very important to them. Likewise, being trusted with work responsibility motivated Gen Y *trusted (handwritten)* members. Many survey respondents (42%) rated responsibility as important to their motivational needs.

The second research question addressed by the researcher in this investigation was *What hygiene factors help motivate Gen Y employees in the workplace?* Herzberg (1968) enumerated the following hygiene factors in his research: personal life, status, supervision, company policy/administration, security, relationships with supervisor, peers, and subordinates, salary, and working condition. Based on the response to this survey, Gen Y students rated personal life, working conditions, and *WC (handwritten)* salary as their top hygiene factors in the workplace.

Survey respondents identified personal life as a highly motivating hygiene factor. Majority of students (73%) strongly believed that their personal life was just as important as their professional life. No students answered that their personal life was of little or no importance to them. The second hygiene factor receiving a high remark was work condition. Most Gen Y students (63%) noted work conditions as very important to their motivational needs. Finally, salary was an important hygiene factor for Gen Y. In the survey, students were asked to rate "How important is your salary to your motivation at work?" Almost half of students (47%) responded salary as important to their work motivation.

The final research question addressed by the researcher in this investigation was What strategies can managers provide to strengthen job satisfaction of Gen Y employees? Based on Gen Y response to the survey, the following strategies can help managers strengthen job satisfaction:

1. Support work/life balance in the workplace – Gen Y clearly believed that their professional life was just as important as their professional life. Potential work/life programs include, but is not limited to, fitness facilities/discount membership, education/training opportunities, flexible working arrangements, family leave policies, and childcare/eldercare programs. Managers and leaders can motivate Gen Y employees by advocating work/life policies/programs in the workplace.

2. Provide Gen Y workers with opportunities to grow in their job – Growing in one's career was important to Gen Y. Managers can provide Gen Y with challenging work as their skill and knowledge progressed.

3. Use achievement as a way to reward/motivate Gen Y workers – When Gen Y achieves at work, managers can motivate Gen Y by using rewards or increased responsibility. For instance, recognition of "employee of the month" award can provide motivation to a Gen Y worker. Managers can customize rewards and incentives to best fit an employee's need (i.e., gift certificates).

4. Create working conditions suited for Gen Y – A safe, comfortable working environment mattered to Gen Y workers. Managers must clearly articulate safety and fun at work to employees. Having a fun and comfortable working environment can greatly motivate Gen Y cohort.

5. Offer increasing responsibilities as a reward – Gen Y workers viewed being trusted with responsibility as a good motivator. Managers can offer increased

responsibility as a reward for an employee's good performance.

6. Create a fair salary/compensation package – Salary was an important motivation to Gen Y. Having a fair salary/compensation structure is an important tool in ensuring Gen Y's motivational needs are met (i.e., pay for performance program).

Limitations and Recommendation for Future Research

Based on their response to the demographic questions, this learner assumed that the respondents to the survey are, in fact, a member of Gen Y cohort. In addition, this learner assumed that participants were answering the survey questions honestly and voluntarily, and thereby providing data, which truly reflected the perceptions of Gen Y cohort.

The main limitation in the methodology was that the study was limited to the perceptions of Gen Y students at the Pacific region of the United States. Some other limitations include: the findings was limited to students who volunteered and completed the surveys; and the instrument used in the study was self-designed questionnaire and its validity may need further examination.

Areas requiring further research include (a) measuring the difference (if any) in hygiene/motivator factors among Gen Y workers; (b) determining if results from a replicated study using respondents who are actually employed agree or disagree with the finding of this study; (c) how motivator and hygiene factors impact Gen Y employees in the workplace.

Conclusion

To the author's knowledge, this study is one of the only few to directly address Gen Y motivational needs utilizing Frederick Herzberg's two-factor theory of motivation (1968). Gen Y workers present the next colossal opportunity and the next significant challenge for managers and business leaders in the new economy. As Gen Y continues to grow and enter the workforce, the need to effectively manage Gen Y employees become paramount for managers and business leaders. This study should help managers and leaders in identifying the motivational and managerial needs of Gen Y workers and should add to the growing body of knowledge on effectively managing and motivating Gen Y workers.

Perhaps the greatest benefit of this study is that it will increase awareness and discussion among managers and business leaders on how to effectively motivate and manage Gen Y members in the workplace. While other theories of motivation may prove useful in exploring workplace motivational and managerial factors of Gen Y workers, this learner was intrigued in the popularity and utility of the two-factor theory among business practitioners.

Within your control — as a
manager, as a Gen Y

PART IV:
25 WAYS TO
MOTIVATE GEN Y
WORKERS

1) Support work/life balance in the workplace

In a recent survey with Gen Y students, Gen Y clearly believed their personal life was just as important as their professional life. Potential work/life programs include, but are not limited to, fitness facilities/discount membership, education/training opportunities, flexible working arrangements, family leave policies, and childcare/eldercare programs. Managers and leaders can motivate Gen Y employees by advocating work/life policies/programs in the workplace.

ACTION STEP:
List the ways I will support work/life balance in the workplace:

_____
_____
_____

2) Provide Gen Y workers with opportunities to grow in their job

Growing in one's career is important to Gen Y. Managers can provide Gen Y with challenging work as their skill and knowledge progressed. Frederick Herzberg, a psychologist who developed the two-factor theory of motivation, indicated that growth is one of the most important motivators for employees.

ACTION STEP:
List the ways I will provide Gen Y workers with opportunities to grow in their job:

_____

_____

_____

_____

_____

3) Use achievement as a way to reward/motivate Gen Y workers

When Gen Y achieves at work, managers can motivate Gen Y by using rewards or increased responsibility. For instance, recognition of "employee of the month" award can provide motivation to a Gen Y worker. Managers can customize rewards and incentives to best fit an employee's need (i.e., gift certificates).

ACTION STEP:
List the ways I will use achievement as a way to reward/ motivate Gen Y workers:

_____

_____

_____

_____

_____

4) Create working conditions suited for Gen Y

A safe, comfortable working environment matter to Gen Y workers. Managers must clearly articulate safety and fun at work to employees. Having a fun and comfortable working environment can greatly motivate Gen Y cohort.

ACTION STEP:
List the ways I will create working conditions suited for Gen Y:

_____

_____

_____

_____

_____

5) Offer increasing responsibilities as a reward

Gen Y workers view being trusted with responsibility as a good motivator. Managers can offer increased responsibility as a reward for an employee's good performance. Gen Yers will feel that their managers have trust and confidence in them and can boost their self-esteem.

ACTION STEP:
List the ways I will offer increasing responsibilities as a reward:

_____

_____

_____

_____

_____

6) Create a fair salary/compensation package

Salary is an important motivator to Gen Y. Having a fair salary/compensation structure is an important tool in ensuring Gen Y's motivational needs are met (i.e., pay for performance program). In this author's survey with Gen Y students, Gen Yers ranked having a good salary as important to their motivational needs. Compensation is not just about money, but can encompass training and other job benefits such as medical and education.

ACTION STEP:
List the ways I will create a fair salary/compensation package:

_____

_____

_____

_____

_____

7) Give them cutting-edge technology

Technology can be a great motivator for Yers. Gen Yers are techno-savvy and have grown up with easy access to technology such as cell phones and the Internet. Providing cutting-edge technology at work can help them do their jobs better and motivate them to perform better.

ACTION STEP:
List the ways I will give Gen Y cutting-edge technology:

_____

_____

_____

_____

_____

8) Provide flexibility in their work.

Job flexibility can be a great motivator for Gen Y employees. Since Gen Yers value both their personal and professional lives, managers who understand and use job flexibility will gain kudos from Gen Yers. As an example, having flexible hours can be motivating to Gen Yers who are fully engaged with both their personal/professional lives.

ACTION STEP:
List the ways I will provide flexibility in their work:

_____
_____
_____
_____
_____

9) Share job knowledge

Gen Y workers value knowledge. Managers who share job knowledge with younger workers will benefit in many ways. Gen Y workers will feel a sense of trust knowing their superiors are keeping them in the loop and sharing job knowledge with them.

ACTION STEP:
List the ways I will share job knowledge:

_____
_____
_____
_____
_____

technology
tacit knowledge

10) Encourage & reward

Managers and business leaders who effectively encourage and reward Gen Y workers will gain a competitive edge in today's globalized workplace. There are many ways to encourage and reward younger workers. For instance, a manager can give his subordinate a day off as a form of recognition.

ACTION STEP:
List the ways I will encourage and reward Gen Y workers:

_____

_____

_____

_____

_____

11) Challenge them

Gen Yers prefer meaningful work that challenges them both personally and professionally. They want to feel they are making a difference to their workplace and society. Managers must challenge workers by giving them work tasks/assignments that challenge them on a daily basis.

ACTION STEP:
List the ways I will challenge Gen Y members:

_____

_____

_____

_____

_____

12) Make work fun

Gen Y workers are fast becoming the dominant player in the workplace. Thus, companies who embrace a fun, rather than conventional company culture create a higher rate of job satisfaction with younger employees. Some great ideas on how to make a "fun" workplace environment include showing humorous movies during lunchtime; sponsoring an "interesting pizza day"; running an "ugly tie/scarf contest," and bringing a massage therapist for a periodic chair massages.

ACTION STEP:
List the ways I will make work fun:

_____

_____

_____

_____

_____

13) Show respect and appreciation

Treating Gen Yers with respect means recognizing they are appreciated and respected as human beings. Gen Yers respect managers who are confident and knowledgeable, who care about them, and who understand the importance of mutual self-respect. Thus, retaining and motivating younger workers means treating them with respect and appreciation.

ACTION STEP:
List the ways I will show respect and appreciation at my workplace:

_____

_____

_____

_____

_____

14) Give frequent feedbacks

Annual or semi-annual performance reviews do not work for Gen Y. This generation wants constant feedbacks. Gen Yers expect managers and supervisors to provide clear and immediate feedback. For instance, spot reviews lead to consistent improvement. Growth and improvement are what matter the most to Gen Y.

ACTION STEP:
List the ways I will give frequent feedbacks:

_____
_____
_____
_____
_____

15) Treat fairly/professionally

Gen Yers want to be treated fairly and professionally in the workplace. The biggest mistake managers can make is to treat them as "teen-agers" or interns. For instance, introducing a Gen Y worker to colleagues as John our "Human Resources Specialist" can go a long way as opposed to intern or subordinate.

ACTION STEP:
List the ways I will treat Gen Y members fairly/professionally:

_____

_____

_____

_____

_____

16) Model expected behavior

Managers and leaders must demonstrate expected behavior to younger workers. All leaders are role models, whether they like it or not. Employees look to their managers and leaders for direction and guidance. Particularly, behaviors that are important to one's organization must be shown on a regular basis. To illustrate, a university in Oregon shuts down once a year so students and staff can volunteer and contribute to service projects around the city.

ACTION STEP:
List the ways I will model expected behavior to Gen Y workers:

_____
_____
_____
_____
_____

17) Train strategically/digitally

Each individual learns in a unique way. Training Gen Yers strategically and effectively using the digital world can benefit organizations. Gen Y grew up with playing video games and are very techno-savvy. Managers who utilize all avenues or resources available to train Gen Yers will gain in the process. For example, combining classroom lectures, and on-the-job training can add value in training younger workers.

ACTION STEP:
List the ways I will train Gen Y strategically/digitally:

_____

_____

_____

_____

_____

18) Provide Ongoing Learning and Development

Gen Yers are the most education-minded generation in history. This "education is cool" generation clearly needs ongoing learning as they progress through their jobs. They seek out creative challenges and view colleagues as vast resources from whom to gain knowledge. Offer programs that will develop their career within the organization such as networking sessions or formal structured courses through external educational providers.

ACTION STEP:
List the ways I will provide ongoing learning and development at my workplace:

_____

_____

_____

_____

_____

19) Encourage collaboration and communication

Encouraging collaboration can play a significant role in improving organization-wide communication. Gen Yers are team players and work well with others. Managers who support teamwork and collaboration will benefit in the long-term vitality of the organization.

ACTION STEP:
List the ways I will encourage collaboration and communication at my workplace:

_____

_____

_____

_____

_____

20) Focus on the meaning and purpose of work

Focus on the purpose and meaning of work when delegating task to Gen Y workers. Gen Yers want to make a difference and a positive impact in the workplace. Managers who explain the importance of a project/task will help Gen Yers find meaning and purpose in their work. This is a great motivational tool for managers to use in delegating tasks.

ACTION STEP:
List the ways I will focus on the meaning and purpose of work with Gen Y workers:

_____
_____
_____
_____
_____

21) Create choices

Everyone makes choices everyday. One-size fits all mentality does not always work in today's globalized marketplace. To retain Gen Yers, creating choices can be a motivator. Whether a choice in many different benefits, working hours, or office layout, customization is the key to retaining and motivating this younger generation.

ACTION STEP:
List the ways I will create choices for Gen Y members at my workplace:

_____
_____
_____
_____
_____

22) Provide mentor

A mentor is someone who serves as a teacher, guide, counselor, or advisor. Gen Y workers are career-oriented and want to succeed. Having a mentor who will guide them through office politics and career progression will a great motivator for Gen Yers. Conversely, Gen Yers are techno-savvy and can show older workers the power of online communities and new technologies.

ACTION STEP:
List the ways I will provide mentor:

_____
_____
_____
_____
_____

23) Create customized career path

Each individual is unique. Thus, customizing a career path for each Gen Y worker can be a motivational tool for managers. Moreover, creating a customized career path will create a sense of control Gen Y desires and will provide them with a realistic account of their progress and their future with an employer. For instance, an entry-level clerk at Wal-Mart can customize his career-path with the company with his supervisor enumerating the ways to be promoted and advance to shift supervisor.

ACTION STEP:
List the ways I will create customized career path for Gen Y employees:

_____

_____

_____

_____

_____

24) Seize formal and informal time-out times

Seizing informal and formal time-out times can make a difference in helping to motivate Gen Yers. Informality facilitates significant sharing which include opportunities to get out of the office to talk (i.e., take Gen Y employee to lunch). Formal time-outs include scheduling one-on-one, work-related sessions with each team member on a consistent basis (i.e., weekly one-hour session with an employee).

ACTION STEP:
List the ways I will seize formal and informal time-outs with Gen Y:

_____
_____
_____
_____
_____

25) Listen to the needs of Gen Y

This is the most important motivational tool for managers—listen to Gen Y! If you ask Gen Yers, they will tell you what motivates them and what turns them off. Hear what Gen Yers have to say—have Gen Yers list what motivates them on paper or create a focus group with Gen Y workers.

ACTION STEP:
List the ways I will listen to the needs of Gen Y members at my workplace:

_____

_____

_____

_____

_____

In Summary...
25 Ways to Motivate Gen Yers

1) Support work/life balance in the workplace
2) Provide Gen Y workers with opportunities to grow in their job
3) Use achievement as a way to reward/motivate Gen Y workers
4) Create working conditions suited for Gen Y
5) Offer increasing responsibilities as a reward
6) Create a fair salary/compensation package
7) Give them cutting-edge technology
8) Provide flexibility in their work
9) Share job knowledge
10) Encourage & reward
11) Challenge them
12) Make work fun
13) Show respect and appreciation
14) Give me frequent feedback
15) Treat fairly/professionally
16) Model expected behavior
17) Train strategically/digitally
18) Need for Ongoing Learning
19) Encourage collaboration
20) Focus on the meaning and purpose of work
21) Create choices
22) Provide mentor
23) Create customized career path
24) Seize informal time-out times
25) Listen to the needs of Gen Y

PART V: CONCLUSION

Gen Yers are making waves! Like it or not, Gen Y workers are here to stay. They are truly the workforce of the future. Gen Y continues to bring new ideas and values into the workplace. Employers across all industries must understand and appreciate the qualities and values of the younger worker in order to recruit, motivate, and retain them. In summary, Gen Yers are highly educated, willing to learn, techno-savvy, and motivated workers. Effectively motivating Gen Y is one of a manager's top duties. Thus, there are many ways to motivate workers, and it is just a matter of finding the right factors that suit an individual.

BIBLIOGRAPHY

Biography.com. (2008). Retrieved January 2, 2008, from http://www.biography.com

Dulin, L. (2005). Leadership preferences of a Generation Y cohort: A mixed method Investigation (Doctoral dissertation, University of North Texas, 2005). *Dissertation Abstracts International, 66/07*, 2633.

Eisner, S. P. (2005, Autumn). Managing generation Y. S.A.M Advanced Management Journal, 70(4), 4-15.

Herzberg, F. (1968, January/February). One more time: How do you motivate employees? Harvard Business Review, 81(1), 87-96.

Janiszewski, R. D. (2004). Motivational factors that influence Baby Boomers versus Generation X: Independent insurance agents (Doctoral dissertation, Capella University, 2004). *Dissertation Abstracts International, 65/09*, 3459.

Lancaster, L., & Stillman, D. (2002). When generations collide: Who they are. Why they clash. How to solve the generational puzzle at work. New York, NY: Collins Business.

Martin, C.A., & Tulgan, B. (2001). Executive summary: Managing the generation mix 2007. Retrieved August 21, 2007, from www.rainmakerthinking.com/mix2007.doc

Maslow, A.H. (1968). Toward a psychology of being (2nd ed.). New York: Van Nostrand.

Meredith, G. E., Schewe, C. D., & Hiam, A. (2002). Managing by defining moments. New York: Hungry Minds.

NAS Insights (2006). Generation Y: The millennials, ready or not, here they come. Retrieved August 30, 2008, from www.nasrecruitment.com/talenttips/NASinsights/GenerationY.pdf

Schlichtemeier-Nutzman, S. E. (2002). Linearity across generations: An exploratory study of training techniques (Doctoral dissertation, The University of Nebraska - Lincoln, 2001). Dissertation Abstracts International, 62/08, 2659.

Smola, K. W., & Sutton, C. D. (2002). Generational differences: Revisiting generational work values for the new millennium. Journal of Organizational Behavior, 23, 363-382.

Strauss, W., & Howe, N. (1991). Generations: The history of America's future, 1584 to 2069. New York: William Morrow.

Vroom, V. (1964). Work and motivation. New York: Wiley.

Wagner, J. A., & Hollenbeck, J. R. (2001). Organizational behavior: Securing a competitive advantage. Forth Worth, TX: Harcourt College Publishers.

Zemke, R., Raines, C., & Filipczak, B. (2000). Generations at work: Managing the clash of Veterans, Boomers, Xers, and Nexters in your workplace. New York, NY: AMACOM.

Lightning Source UK Ltd.
Milton Keynes UK
05 January 2011

165211UK00001B/99/P

9 781440 105449